A Parent's Guide to
BUILDING WINNERS
Through Athletics

BARRY PATTERSON

outskirts press

A Parent's Guide for Building Winners Through Athletics
All Rights Reserved.
Copyright © 2019 Barry Patterson
v2.0

The opinions expressed in this manuscript are solely the opinions of the author and do not represent the opinions or thoughts of the publisher. The author has represented and warranted full ownership and/or legal right to publish all the materials in this book.

This book may not be reproduced, transmitted, or stored in whole or in part by any means, including graphic, electronic, or mechanical without the express written consent of the publisher except in the case of brief quotations embodied in critical articles and reviews.

Outskirts Press, Inc.
http://www.outskirtspress.com

ISBN: 978-1-9772-0741-8

Cover Photo © 2019 www.gettyimages.com. All rights reserved - used with permission.

Outskirts Press and the "OP" logo are trademarks belonging to Outskirts Press, Inc.

PRINTED IN THE UNITED STATES OF AMERICA

Table of Contents

Let's Have Fun! 1
Positive Is Powerful 3
Effort and Attitude Are Everything 5
Know Your Athlete's Ability Level 7
Lead by Example 8
Successful Failures 9
Raising Good Teammates 11
Teachable Moments 14
Know and Understand What Your Child Wants Out of Athletics 16
Guiding a Gifted Athlete 18
Balancing Act 20
Delayed Communication 21
Pushing Athletes 23
Find a Mentor 25
Parents Will Be Inconvenienced 27
Choose Your Words Wisely 28
Developmental Differences 30
Avoid Talking about Coaches 31
Be Their Biggest Fan 33
Respect the Coach 35

Coachable Kids	38
Respecting Sports Officials	40
Finish What You Start	42
Hold Your Athlete Accountable	44
Give Them Some Independence	46
Shoot for the Stars	48
Let Athletes Be Athletes	50
Transferable Skills	52
Confidence: I Don't Think I Can, I Know I Can	53
Encourage Leadership	55
Body Language Speaks Loudly	57
Little Things Make a Big Difference	59
Controlling Emotions	61
Thinking before Reacting	63
Do the Math	66
What Are College Coaches Looking For?	68
Start Thinking about College	71
Scholarship Information	73
College Athletic Scholarship Limits for Men 2018–19	75
College Athletic Scholarship Limits for Women 2018–19	77
NCAA Division I Academic Requirements	79
NCAA Division II Academic Requirements	84
NCAA Division III	88
NAIA Academic Requirements	89
NJCAA Academic Requirements	90
All Sports Experiences Will End Sooner or Later	91

I have been involved in athletics in some way for forty-five years. I started as a young athlete playing every sport possible. I loved to compete, and my parents were very supportive of my endeavors. They would haul me around to practice and competitions all over Oklahoma. My parents were involved in athletics as well, and they enjoyed watching me compete. They were good, sports-minded people who held me accountable as an athlete and helped instill in me a quality work ethic in everything I did. I was a three sport athlete through high school competing in football, baseball and wrestling. I was good at football and baseball, but wrestling was my passion. I was a state champion in 1984 and wrestled at Northeastern Oklahoma A&M Junior College for two years. I married my wife of over thirty years after my sophomore year in college, and shortly afterward we started a family. As I was going through college, I worked part-time for our local sports recreational center. Anytime they were short a coach, the youth center director would volunteer me for the experience. Looking back, I had no idea what I was doing, but I had one thing going my way: I cared about kids. I had a great athletic experience growing up, and I wanted the youth of Cushing, Oklahoma to have a great experience also. Initially, as a family provider, I felt I needed to make lots of money, and I was always good with numbers, so I graduated from Oklahoma State University with a degree in finance. However, it didn't take me long to realize my passion was athletics, so I went back to school to get my certification in business education.

I started coaching in the fall of 1991 in my hometown of Cushing. I coached junior high football, wrestling, and track. I coached in Cushing for two years, and then I took a head wrestling coach position in Vinita, Oklahoma. I coached in Vinita for three years, and then I had the opportunity to go back home to Cushing. I coached in Cushing from 1995 to 2009. I was fortunate to have coached some outstanding teams and some outstanding individuals during my career. Cushing wrestling won six dual state titles and three traditional state titles during my coaching career. In 2009, I took over as Cushing High School athletic director. I have been the athletic director ever since.

I have always strongly encouraged students to participate in athletics because athletics has so much to offer young people. Athletics provides a fun, challenging way for youth to learn lessons that will benefit them in all areas of life for years to come. However, with 70 percent of our youth quitting athletics before the age of thirteen—and the way some athletes, coaches, and parents show poor sportsmanship at sporting events— it makes me wonder if we are missing the target in athletics. Are the kids learning life lessons through athletics? If so, are they the right lessons?

I believe in athletics, and I still think there are many more positives than negatives when it comes to athletics. I personally have made many mistakes as a coach, and as a parent, but like a successful athlete I turned my mistakes into positive failures. I have learned from my mistakes and corrected them along the way to provide a better experience for the athletes I coached and my own children in their athletic endeavors.

As a father of three boys, I wanted to be the best father possible, and I wanted my sons to be passionate about athletics as I was and still am today. So when my boys were very young, I started to pay attention to how parents responded to their kids in athletics. I started to notice some common traits of parents whose kids worked hard, were respectful, and competed to their ability. I took mental notes on how most of these parents were heavily involved in an encouraging way. Most of the parents held their kids accountable, and thus the kids held themselves accountable.

The objective of each athletic experience should be to become a *winner* by being involved in athletics. Obviously, that doesn't mean every athlete is going to win in their athletic endeavors, but by providing a positive athletic support system, it can be an experience that gives them the qualities that enable them to *win* in life. This is a guide to help parents aid their young athletes in reaching their full potential.

It is important that you find that balance as an athlete's parent to provide them with quality support, without going overboard to the point that you take away the enjoyment and the very important life lessons your athlete should be learning through organized sports. Today parents seem to push their children to excel in athletics like never before. Parents have their athletes practice for hours daily, they provide them with individual lessons, they hire personal trainers, and they put them on traveling teams so they can maximize their potential. However, many times it is one step forward and two steps back. The way many parents handle their child's athletic experience is counterproductive. There are a lot of very good parents who are making very poor decisions when it comes to their children's athletic experiences. Parents need to understand the big picture. Have patience, think things through, and don't get caught up in doing what everyone else is doing. It is also important to understand that each child is unique, and what worked with one may not work with the other. As a parent you have to know your child and what motivates them.

There are more kids participating in youth athletics today than ever before, but unfortunately the retention rate is not good. As stated earlier, statistics show that over 70 percent will quit by the age of thirteen. I think there are many reasons for this alarming number of young kids dropping out of athletics. Parents today don't want their children to experience any kind of disappointment, rejection, or discomfort. Athletics provides plenty of disappointment, rejection, and discomfort. We have many young children who are missing out on a great opportunity to learn how to deal with these situations at a young age so they are prepared for better handling these feelings in life situations as adults. Another problem with our youth is they live in a society of instant gratification. Some kids have never been in situations where the payoff is down the road. Athletics offers the perfect venue for them to learn delayed gratification. As a parent, it is important that you are part of the solution and not the problem. If you want your children to have a positive athletic experience, they need your help. Obviously, following this advice will not guarantee your child an athletic scholarship. However, I believe it will increase their odds of having a positive athletic experience, learning life lessons along the way, and reaching their full athletic potential. Always remember your child's success in athletics does not indicate what kind of parent you are, but having a child who is coachable, respectful, resilient, a good teammate, and always tries his or her hardest is a direct reflection of your parenting.

The following information is presented in an order from youth athletics through high school athletics.

Let's Have Fun!

Athletics should be fun. As a matter of fact, having fun is the number one reason why kids participate in sports. Especially at a young age, the emphasis should be on learning the fundamentals of the sport and having a good time with their peers. Many have the perception that you have to win in athletics in order for kids at any age to have fun. However, many times it's just the opposite. Kids who have a good time have a better attitude about the sport and thus are more likely to be successful. When kids are very young, I think they should be in less-demanding leagues with fewer competitions where winning is not emphasized. Hopefully your child will enjoy their first experience with Little League athletics and develop a passion for the sport. That passion will enable them to transition a little later when athletics starts to get a little more serious and competitive. As your athlete gets older, they should experience more demanding practices as they condition their bodies and refine their skills, but this can be fun as well. When kids are having fun, they have a tendency to work harder, focus more, and have more success. Success is determined partially by the athlete's desire to succeed, which comes from the athlete's love of the sport. Some may watch a practice and say, "How could all that work be fun?" When athletes get older, success sometimes means pushing yourself past your comfort zone in order to improve your game. Most athletes enjoy this phase of striving for success. My most enjoyable athletic experiences have been when I was involved with teams that worked extremely hard to achieve a common goal and when camaraderie developed from working hard with my peers.

It should be one of the parents' goals pertaining to their children's involvement in athletics to make sure they are having a good time. Some ways that parents can increase the odds of their children having enjoyment in athletics are the following: being positive, being encouraging instead of demanding, being open to fun rather than emphasizing success, and being a positive role model. Most children will follow the lead of their parents. For example, if you say, "I love watching you play" or "Have fun playing," the athletes are much more likely to have an enjoyable experience. This doesn't mean that there will not be difficult times for your child in athletics, but overall it should be a good experience.

Parents should focus on having fun as well. Enjoy the journey. Focus on the little victories. Parents should realize that their children grow up very fast, and they should always try to make great memories.

Just play. Have fun. Enjoy the game. —Michael Jordan

Positive Is Powerful

In order for kids to maximize their potential in athletics, it is important that they have a positive support system. Positive parenting is one of the most important factors in assuring that your child has a good athletic experience. Parents should encourage and inspire. Positive parents raise confident children. Positive parents are essential for the young athlete to get off to a good start. Statements like "I am so proud of you" or "You were awesome" will make a huge impact on your child. Sometimes parents have to look for the small victories or improvements; however, if you as the parent stay positive, the small victories will start to add up. Kids are more likely to succeed when they feel good about themselves and are having fun. Remember, your comments become your child's inner voice. You want their inner voice saying, "I think I can, I think I can," and that will eventually turn into "I know I can, I know I can." Immediate feedback always works best.

Athletes whose parents are negative rarely reach their full potential. The negative outlook will carry over to the athlete, and eventually the athlete will become negative toward the coaches and teammates and can poison the entire team with that attitude. Negative comments over an extended period of time cause doubt, frustration, jealousy, shame, sadness, and fear. Negative comments will cause negative emotions, and this process will lead to creating an underachiever. Many times players who are surrounded by negative comments are fine if everything is going well, but when things get tough, these athletes have a tendency to quit competing hard and give up.

Positive comments over an extended period of time will cause inspiration, confidence, joy, optimism, and excitement. Positive comments will cause positive emotions and lead to creating an overachiever. These athletes compete hard regardless of the situation.

So how do you handle your child after a very poor performance? Many times you can still find the positives, such as hustle, effort, and attitude (things the athlete can and should control). An understanding parent who stays optimistic is also needed after a rough outing.

The best way to raise positive children in a negative world is to have positive parents who love them unconditionally and serve as excellent role models. —Zig Ziglar

Effort and Attitude Are Everything

Ask any coach, and they will list effort and attitude as top characteristics they like to see in their athletes. Effort and attitude should be emphasized in youth sports and hopefully become positive habits for your athlete throughout their careers. Unfortunately, many parents and coaches have the "win at all costs" mentality. We live in a society that focuses on results and winning. The win at all costs mentality puts a lot of pressure on the athlete. If you encourage your child to not worry about the wins, and focus instead on having a great attitude and playing hard from whistle to whistle, success on and off the field will take care of itself.

It is important that parents and athletes understand that many times you can perform up to your ability and still lose the competition. This effort obviously deserves positive feedback. Likewise, you can win a competition and perform poorly. If your children are in athletics long enough, they are going to have bad outings, and that is okay as long as the effort and attitude are there.

Athletic competitions offer a great venue for learning some important life lessons. One of those lessons is only worry about the things you can control (effort and attitude), and don't waste time worrying about what you can't control (officiating, what opponents do, etc.).

The only disability in life is a bad attitude. —Scott Hamilton

Know Your Athlete's Ability Level

This is difficult for most parents because as parents we see our children a little differently. We are so proud of them, and we want them to succeed in all they do, so we visualize them with optimistic eyes. Most parents think their children are better than what they are, especially when the athlete has worked very hard toward something. Many parents have unrealistic goals for their athletes. Unfortunately the parents who set unrealistic goals for their children are setting them up to fail. Young kids will work hard to please their parents, but if the expectation level is out of reach, both parent and child will be disappointed. High expectations can cause long-term relationship issues between the adult and the athlete. Be realistic about your child's ability level. The goal should be for the athlete to reach his or her own potential.

Also, parents should look at the big picture and focus on the process. It's not where they are in T-ball that matters; it's how they progress and develop that counts most. The process of developing as an athlete is a marathon not a sprint. Keep your athlete excited about the process by recognizing their small successes along the way.

The path of development is a journey of discovery that is clear only in retrospect, and it's rarely a straight line.
—*Eileen Kennedy-Moore*

Lead by Example

Every time you say something or react to a situation, your child is watching you. Understand that your child looks up to you, and you are their role model. This is a great responsibility. Parents should exhibit the sportsmanship qualities they want their children to possess. Character development should be one of the primary goals for your child to get out of athletics, and you have the ability to make this happen as a good role model. With this in mind, it is very important that you treat people (coaches, your athlete, other athletes, officials, other parents) with respect. As a parent you should also model all the qualities during your everyday life that you want your children to get out of athletics: work ethic, resilience, humility, commitment, discipline, patience, confidence, and sportsmanship. The more you demonstrate these characteristics, the greater chance your children will exhibit them as well. Your children are following your lead. If you act negatively and blame others, your children are likely to do the same. If your child is acting this way, not only are they showing poor sportsmanship, but it is negatively affecting their athletic performance and their team culture as well.

Don't worry that children never listen to you;
worry that they are always watching.
—Robert Fulghum

Successful Failures

I think this is one of the most misunderstood areas in athletics. As parents we want our children to be successful in all they do, but some kids miss out on one of the most important processes. In order for athletes to better their skills, develop mental toughness (grit), and learn how to compete, they must learn from adversity. We don't like to see our children fail, but it is extremely important if you want them to maximize their potential as athletes that you understand your role as a parent in this process.

Losing games, getting along with teammates, getting through tough practices, sitting on the bench, and dealing with injuries are just a few of the adversities that athletes will face. Responding, adapting, and dealing with all of this will be the solid foundation the athlete can pull from later in life.

Don't make excuses for their performance. If you do, you will create an athlete who will always underachieve. They will fall in line with the parents and start making excuses for their shortcomings. When these athletes are in a situation that requires their competitive juices to come out, they will know in the back of their mind that if they come up short, there will be a way to justify their failure to succeed.

Stress that it is okay to fail, and if you handle it correctly and teach them to handle it correctly, they can learn from their shortcomings and continue to grow and get better from each scenario. Athletes need to know that failing is okay. Failure is inevitable. Everyone fails at times in life, but it is those who remain focused on their goals and learn from their mistakes that become successful at their particular endeavor. "Successful failures" are failures your athlete will learn from. Don't deprive them of this great teaching tool. A winner believes all problems have solutions. Failures, setbacks, and mistakes only make them wiser and stronger for future successes. If you can communicate to your athlete to always play hard and not worry about making mistakes, they will become more resilient. If they make an error in a baseball game, they are able to shake it off, come back, and make the next play. We have all seen players who are really good when things are going well, but the minute something bad happens they seem to fall apart. They worry about the last mistake, and all of a sudden they make another and then another. Parents have the ability to control this meltdown by not emphasizing mistakes in their performance. Emphasize the hustle, focus, and playing hard.

If young athletes continue to compete hard, have the attitude that they will learn from their mistakes, and continue to improve as an athlete, they will be successful.

Confidence is one of the most important attributes to being successful in life, and the best way to develop confidence in your children is to allow them to fail without making excuses for them. After they have been knocked down, encourage them to get back up and continue working on their skills. Eventually they will start to overcome, and their confidence will soar.

Adversity causes some men to break, others to break records.
—William A. Ward

Raising Good Teammates

Teaching your child to work with others to achieve a common goal is a great learning tool that will greatly benefit them on an athletic team, in the workforce, and throughout life. Teach them that you win as a team, lose as a team, and get better as a team.

It seems so many athletes will beat their chest when things are going good, but when the tide turns and times are tough, the same athletes are the first to point their finger and blame someone else. There is no place for individualism in team sports.

Great coaches seem to be really good at getting individuals to work together to reach team goals. I think some parents are equally good, and they see the many long-term advantages of teaching their children to work together for a cause. This will help them later in life in their marriage, in their job, and in their community.

As parents you can help this team-first mentality by avoiding certain comments like "Wow, you scored twenty points." This type of comment can create a selfish player. Your athlete will likely associate his point production with praise and start shooting the ball even when he is not open. Obviously this type of individualism goes against the team concept. "Wow, you scored all four touchdowns" makes it sound as if the young athlete did all the work when actually he had lots of help from the other ten players on the field.

Encouraging statements like "You competed very hard; I am so proud of you" or "Great hustle" or "You were so focused" are much better. Praise your athlete for his or her effort and tenacity.

Many times athletes can have a tremendous game and not score any points, touchdowns, or runs. If you only praise the production, it can send the young athlete the wrong message.

Many parents and athletes think high school athletes have to have their numbers (stats) in order to get a college scholarship, that they have to get so many touchdowns or score so many points to get noticed. However, the reality is college coaches, just like high school coaches, want team-oriented players. College coaches are looking for selfless players who will fit into their system. As a parent, don't get caught up in numbers or stats. Focus your praise on hustle, effort, and helping the team. It is also beneficial to praise your athlete's teammates for helping your athlete be successful. "Your teammates blocked great for you, and you made some really good runs."

Teach your child to know and understand their role on the team. Teamwork works best when all of the players know their role and focus on doing their job. It is important for parents to convey the message to their athletes that the nonstarters also have an extremely important role on the team. They need to be ready to compete when their number is called to go into the game. Nonstarters are important role players in practice as well. Many times the nonstarters' roles are to make the starters better in practice. An encouraging and supporting nonstarter can multiply the success of the starter. Athletes should embrace their role and continue to try to improve individually to contribute even more to the team in the future.

Teach your athletes to encourage and inspire their teammates. They should accept the abilities of their teammates and work as a unit to maximize their potential. Teach them that attitude, effort, and teamwork are contagious, and they can set the standard for the other players to follow. Individualism can tear a team down much faster than teamwork and unity can build a team up.

As a parent you can model teamwork by getting involved and helping the team. Volunteer at the concession stand or work on fundraisers. There are usually several ways that parents can be involved with the team.

Good players inspire themselves; great players inspire others.
—Unknown

Teachable Moments

As parents you should always look for teachable moments in your child's athletic experiences. Try to find times during your child's activities where they display the following character traits: hardworking, coachable, persistent, resilient, sportsmanlike, and accountable, as well as many others. It is a great opportunity for parents to point out the times when their athlete displayed these valuable traits. Doing this will raise the athlete's confidence level. All of these traits are 100 percent controllable by the athlete. Focusing on praising the areas in which the athlete has control over will increase the self-esteem of the athlete.

It is also a good idea to watch athletic events on TV with your child. In every game you will be able to find some teachable moments. It may be a case where a professional football player demonstrates unsportsmanlike behavior. As a parent you have the opportunity to explain to your athlete the reasons why the behavior was unacceptable. You may be watching a professional baseball game where a player misses a ground ball, but the next time the ball is hit to him, he makes an outstanding play. This is a great opportunity to talk to your athlete about the player's ability to forget about the mistake and come back and make the next play. You will be surprised after doing this a few times how young kids will pick up on it, and before long they will start pointing out the teachable moments to you.

Storytelling or teachable moments provide us with a vast reference base of real life antidotes for possible future problems. They not only entertain and give us a resource of proven solutions, but they also help shape and mold our character. Therefore, when we don't take our time to communicate with our kids, we rob them of critical life lessons that we and our forefathers learn the hard way—lessons that they would needlessly have to learn through trial and error themselves.
—*Drexel Deal*

Know and Understand What Your Child Wants Out of Athletics

It is very important that you know and understand why your child wants to participate in athletics. Many times what the athlete wants out of the experience and what the parents of the athlete want out of athletics are not the same. What the athlete wants should always trump what the parents want. After all, the athletes are the ones who are going to practice and put in the time. There are many reasons why kids choose to participate in athletics, from wanting to be the best ever to just wanting to be part of a team.

Many parents face the dilemma over whether to put their child in a recreation league or on a traveling team. You should always seek communication from your child on what they want to do. If the parents place them on a traveling baseball team that plays sixty games a summer, and the child was lukewarm on baseball to start with, that will probably be the end of his career. If this same player had two more years to develop at his own pace playing recreation baseball, he may be more ready for travel ball at that time. Let the athletes make the call.

As your child gets older, know what his or her goals are for athletics. Encourage them to set challenging but realistic goals and then work toward achieving those goals. As parents, it is also important that your goals for them fall in line with the goals your children set for themselves.

KNOW AND UNDERSTAND WHAT YOUR CHILD WANTS OUT OF ATHLETICS

Parents should not discourage their child from participating in athletics because they lack athletic ability. They may never receive an athletic scholarship, win a state championship, or even start for a varsity team. But they still learn teamwork, perseverance, responsibility, and commitment; gain confidence and a work ethic; and most importantly, have fun competing with their peers.

I think that the best thing we can do for our children is to allow them to do things for themselves, allow them to be strong, allow them to experience life on their own terms, allow them to take the subway… let them be better people, let them believe more in themselves. — C. JoyBell C.

Guiding a Gifted Athlete

We have all witnessed outstanding youth athletes who look like they should be playing in a different league from the rest of their peers. They are naturally gifted, and all of the athletic qualities come easily for them. Most parents who have kids with great abilities focus more on their results and credentials, which can be a big mistake in the long run. Parents must always communicate effort and good attitude with continued success. If parents communicate to their athletes that they are "the best" as young, gifted athletes, it will take the work ethic, attitude, and many other important qualities for future success out of the equation. When the other athletes begin to close the gap as they mature, the athlete who has always been gifted will get frustrated and will not know how to respond. However, if you communicate to your athlete that "if you work really hard and maintain a positive attitude, you can be a great athlete when you get older," the athlete is more likely to continue to be successful as he or she matures.

A mismanaged athlete who was very gifted as a young competitor can be a nightmare for a high school coach. Many times the athlete isn't used to working hard to get their results, and many times they have a negative attitude. Because of this, their results in high school don't match their performance in Little League. All the parents see is "Johnny was the best in third grade, but now he's not starting? What is going on? The coaches must not be doing their job."

Parents should also stress to their gifted athletes the importance of mastering the basic skills of the sport. Many gifted athletes lack the strong base of fundamentals of the sport because they have always relied on being bigger, faster, and stronger than the other athletes.

*Don't measure yourself by what you have accomplished, but
by what you should have accomplished with your ability.
—John Wooden*

Balancing Act

You have to be very careful with young kids to make sure they have balance in their life. Sometimes they just need to be kids. They need to have time to play and spend time with family. If young athletes are playing sixty baseball games during the summer, they may be missing out on some of the summer fun that other kids are having. If they are not allowed to swim on game days, they are missing out on fun with their friends. I know there are sacrifices that have to be made in order to be successful at anything, but I believe you have to allow young children to do other fun things as well. When they get a little older, the nature of athletics will become a little more demanding, and more sacrifices will have to be made. When they become involved in school athletics, it will become very important that they learn to find balance between all of their activities and academics. Many struggle to find the appropriate balance between academics and athletics. As much as they want to do it all, they have to realize that everyone needs a break. So make sure your athlete has a little down time as well.

Survey after survey indicates that one of the greatest challenges faced by most people is life balance. People tend to focus so much on work and other pressing activities that the relationships and activities they really treasure most end up getting squeezed and pushed aside. —Stephen R. Covey

Delayed Communication

Learn how to approach your athlete after a disappointing situation. All kids are different. However, most need a cooling-down phase before they settle down enough to focus in on any conversation.

Most athletes need time to mentally process the game and handle their emotions. I highly recommend parents give their child some breathing room to soak in the situation and calm down so they can communicate with a clear mind. When you do talk to them about the competition, make sure you and your athlete separate their self-worth from their performance. They need to know that you love them the same regardless of the outcome of the competition. Also, many times it is not what you say to them but how you act. If your athlete struggled in a competition and you give them the silent treatment all the way home, they may sense your disappointment. You should stress that all you expect is their top effort and a good attitude.

Always encourage your child to reflect on the experience and problem-solve for future events. This process teaches young athletes resilience. They also learn not only to work hard, but also to work smart to figure out their weaknesses and try to correct them.

If you give advice during this time, make sure it is not contradictory to what the coach is telling your athlete. You will need to know your athlete and understand how they respond to talking about their situation. With some athletes, the more you talk about a problem with their game, the more they worry about their performance. The more they worry, the more they struggle. Always try to start and end your conversations with them by pointing out the positives: "You continue to improve each game" or "I loved the way you competed." This will allow the athlete to be more open to constructive criticism of their game. Although I am a strong believer in a cooling-off phase before any type of critiquing, I think any form of unsportsmanlike behavior should be nipped immediately. They need to understand that it will not be tolerated.

Every day is a new opportunity. You can build on yesterday's success or put its failures behind and start over again. That's the way life is, with a new game every day, and that's the way baseball is.—Bob Feller

Pushing Athletes

Many parents fall into the trap (and it is a trap) of keeping up with the Joneses. We sometimes see parents push their young athletes very hard. Parents may brag about their athlete playing one hundred baseball games during the summer or going to wrestling tournaments every weekend for four months. Many times these young athletes peak because of the accelerated plan their parents have them on. Other parents see the success these athletes are having, playing every competition possible, and they think their athlete has to do the same to keep pace with the best athletes. So the parents start taking their athletes to extra practices, private lessons, and more competitive travel teams. Sometimes you will see an immediate improvement in your athlete, but after an extended period, many athletes start to get tired. Their body has no time to recover because of the constant training and overtraining. Many times these athletes burn out. I don't like to use the term "burnout," but the kids have been pushed so hard that they don't want to do it anymore. After a couple of years, the retention rate on this type of athlete is much lower than their peers who participated in some competitions but were allowed to be kids and have fun as well.

It is important to note that your child may not have an interest in athletics. It is important that you don't force sports on them. Allow them to find their passion in life. Forcing kids to participate in sports can negatively impact their emotional development. When children lack ability or interest in a sport and are forced to compete, they may be placed in humiliating situations where they continue to fail. Continuous failures can negatively affect the self-esteem of the child. Remember, there are many activities that provide very similar life lessons as athletics provide. Children usually gravitate naturally toward the activities that interest them.

Remember, 70 percent of athletes quit by the age of thirteen, and parents pushing them too hard is one of the primary reasons for such a high rate. Many parents' strong demands ruin their children's athletic experience and many times damage the parent/child relationship permanently.

Sports teaches you character, it teaches you to play by the rules, it teaches you to know what it feels like to win and lose. It teaches you about life. — Billie Jean King

Find a Mentor

Being the parent of an athlete is a very tough job. It is a job that will ultimately involve making some tough decisions with your child concerning his or her athletic experiences. It is always a good idea to find a mentor to lean on for advice. Your mentor should be someone you greatly respect and who has a history of making good decisions. Your mentor should have had positive experiences with their children going through the athletic ranks. I had several people whom I called on for advice, and as my children moved on, I gladly passed the advice on to those who asked me for help. It isn't necessary that your mentor be an expert at the sport your child participates in; many times you may know much more than your mentor about the particular sport. However, the mentor should be able to give you some helpful advice on how to best handle your child through the process.

I think if you look back at each phase of your life and the first time you tried a particular act, it probably wasn't your most successful effort. You probably look back on several of those situations and think, "If I had it to do over again…," I would do this or I would do that. Your children are way too important to make these kinds of mistakes. I know I made plenty of mistakes as a young parent and a young coach. However, I learned from the early mistakes I made. As a young parent, you don't want to make mistakes and learn as you go because you lack resources to help you make the most of your child's athletic experience. This is the very reason you should find a good, positive mentor who can give you valuable advice along the way.

Once you embrace the absolute truth that every leader needs a mentor, you can begin to achieve the massive growth and success that you seek. —Clay Clark

Parents Will Be Inconvenienced

Being a sports parent can be very demanding. You have practice and games. Sometimes it seems all you do is drive your athlete around. At times you wonder if it is worth all the effort and money it takes for your athlete to participate in sports. Your child is definitely worth the investment. Athletics can be a great family activity. This gives you and your child the chance to experience something together and gives you an opportunity to bond with your child.

You need to view your time, money, and commitment in your child as an investment in their life. The interest you receive from your investment comes in the form of the life skills (discipline, mental toughness, work ethic, resilience, and confidence) your child is learning through athletics. Your time, money, and commitment are not an investment in a scholarship, and if you view it that way, chances are you are going to be very disappointed.

What's a good investment? Go home from work early and spend the afternoon throwing a ball around with your son.
—Ben Stein

Choose Your Words Wisely

The words you speak each day are very powerful. Positive words and statements will build self-esteem, and negative words or statements will destroy self-esteem. Many parents say things without even realizing the statements could have an effect on their child. Choose words that are going to build them up and give them confidence.

As a parent, if you make statements like "That team sucks; you guys are going to smash them," you are setting your athlete up to be less focused, and they may underperform according to their potential. I'm sure we can all think of games we have participated in or watched on TV where there was a heavily favored team that looked flat or complacent, and they lost to an inferior team. More than likely the team listened to everyone tell them how bad their opponent was all week. Encourage your athlete to treat every opponent with respect and always prepare for the game in the same way mentally.

You also want to avoid statements like "Wow, this team is awesome! We are in trouble." This can be intimidating, especially for young athletes. You would be surprised by how parents' statements affect their athletes' performance or in some cases lack of performance.

Parents should refrain from bragging too much about their children as well. Bragging parents can put a tremendous amount of pressure on the athletes to live up to high expectations. Many times this will cause the athlete to be afraid to fail, which can affect the way they

CHOOSE YOUR WORDS WISELY

normally play the game. Obviously positive comments and encouragement are great, but excessive bragging can put additional pressure on your athlete.

I have heard parents who were talking about a wrestling tournament explain the athlete's results as "We beat the kid from Texas, and we beat the kid from Kansas, but Johnny lost to the kid from Missouri. He just didn't wrestle very well in that match." This sends the message to the athlete that the parents attach themselves to the successes, but the failures are all on the athlete.

You don't have to watch what you say if you watch what you think. — Bill Johnson

Developmental Differences

Parents should understand developmental differences between athletes. Some athletes develop much faster than their peers.

Strength and speed are very important in athletics. Some kids are much smaller and weaker when they start athletics at a young age. This may limit their success, but they should be encouraged to continue to participate. Their size and ability can change in a hurry.

As mentioned earlier, it is vital to stress the importance of work ethic and attitude to athletes who experience a lot of success at an early age. For those athletes who are late bloomers, it is important that you are positive and patient with them. Many times this type of athlete has naturally developed a strong work ethic and excellent skill just trying to keep up with the more mature athletes at an early age. So when they do mature, they really take off and excel athletically.

Don't compare your athlete to others. It is okay to appreciate the skills and talents of other players, but don't compare your child to the higher-skilled athlete in front of your child. Appreciate your child for his or her unique abilities.

Patience is not simply the ability to wait; it's how we behave while we're waiting. —Joyce Meyer

Avoid Talking about Coaches

One of the biggest problems in athletics today is that parents complain and put down their child's coach right in front of their child. The worst thing a parent can do is take shots at the coach, criticizing decisions and complaining about how the coach handles athletes. This plants the seed that the coach is not treating them fairly, and because their parents are open about it, it is okay for the athlete to complain about this situation openly with other teammates. This type of behavior not only robs the athlete of a positive sports experience, but it also has the potential to poison the entire team. Parents should be respectful of the player/coach relationship. This would be no different from parents grounding their child because of poor grades, and the coach ranting to the player about the poor judgment of the parents to choose to ground the child. Obviously, that would be wrong, and the coach should never do that, just as it would be wrong for the parent to disparage the coach in front of their child. Don't put your athlete in a negative situation between the people they should respect.

In order for your athlete to reach their potential, it is very important that they have a good relationship with their coaches. If a parent talks negatively about the coaches, it could damage the trust and relationship they have with current coaches and even future coaches. Support the coach, and stand behind his or her decision.

Negative people seem to attract other negative people. You can see it at the events. If someone has an issue with the coach, that person seems to find others who have issues, and they complain about the coach the entire game. You may say, "Well, maybe it is the coach that is the common problem." Sometimes it might be, but from my experience the same people do it game after game, regardless of who the coach might be. The sad part is many athletes work hard every day in practice to build their team unity, only to have their negative parents tear it back down.

The sign of great parenting is not the child's behavior. The sign of great parenting is the parent's behavior.
—Andy Smithson

Be Their Biggest Fan

I know it is your parental instinct to want to help your child be successful, but parents should not coach from the stands. Be the best fan you can be. You should cheer and encourage, but refrain from coaching. Parents yelling instructions from the stands can be very confusing for a young athlete, especially if the parent is yelling something different from what the coach expects the child to do. This can result in the athlete feeling torn between the parent and the coach, which makes the child confused. This negatively affects their performance, and their confidence takes a big hit. If the athlete is listening to the parent instead of the coach, it will cause an issue with the coach. Many sports require very quick response time, and your yelling can interfere with their focus. By the time your athlete reacts to what you are saying, it may not be the right thing to do anymore. Encourage your young athlete to pay attention to their coach, and you focus on being the number one fan.

Many parents were coaches at one time, but now their athletes have moved up to school athletics. Parents need to realize that now they have moved into an equally important role as a supporter. If you as a parent are knowledgeable of the sport, there will be time after the competition for you to give them valuable instructions. However, make sure the instructions are consistent with the coach's expectations.

Making sure the youths are learning and having fun is the key. Parents have to remember that the game isn't about them. — Unknown

Respect the Coach

This is where many parents struggle and thus negatively impact the small window of opportunity their child has to participate in organized sports. There should be a mutual respect between the parent and coach. It is in this environment of mutual respect that the athlete will thrive.

Most of the time the coaches are doing what they think is best for the team and the program. The coaches are at every practice and should be good at evaluating talent and work ethic. Coaches should have long-term goals and a vision of how to get there. Parents, many times, are selfish when it comes to their athlete and are not always realistic with their athlete's abilities. Here are a few suggestions on dealing with these situations:

1. Never vent your frustrations with the coach in front of your athlete. Don't sour that relationship.

2. If your athlete is the one who has an issue with the coach, he or she should be the one who discusses the situation with the coach at the appropriate time. One of the biggest lessons you can teach your child is how to have an adult conversation with an authority figure. The situation should be discussed maturely and the final decision from the coach accepted.

3. Always have a cool-down time before you discuss any negative situation with the coach. Right after the game is not a good time. It puts both parties in an awkward position that you may regret at a later time. You should give the situation at least twenty-four hours before making contact with the coach.

4. Make sure you go through the proper chain of command. It is always best to communicate directly with the coach before going to anyone else. Also, parents should communicate in person. Face-to-face meetings are much more effective than a text or phone call.

5. As a parent always refrain from using social media to vent your frustrations. This will only place a multiplier on the problem and will generally embarrass your athlete.

As a parent you should always stress to your children the importance of being respectful to the adults in their life, such as parents, teachers, and coaches.

All coaches have their strengths and weaknesses, and no coach is perfect. I realize there are coaches who lack knowledge of a sport, lack communication skills, and sometimes lack in other areas. However, the vast majority care greatly about the youth, or they wouldn't put themselves in that position to be criticized and ridiculed by parents and fans. I had over twenty different coaches during my playing career, and obviously some were much better than others. However, I learned something I was able to use in my life from each one. I think the multitude of coaches with different philosophies, attitudes, and ways of doing things helped me become a better, more well-rounded coach and person. Although your child's coach may not have the greatest tactical skills, he or she may be exceptional at developing a mental edge. Certain coaches have a talent for instilling confidence and mental toughness that will be instrumental in the athlete's development throughout their athletic career.

In life your children will likely experience many different supervisors during their work careers, and they will have to learn how to make the most of each situation. Let them get used to that experience early, and allow them to handle any situations they have directly with their coach—with you, the parent, remaining on the sidelines. Obviously there are some situations that would be an exception to this rule and may need to be addressed by the parents, but these situations are rare.

Growth is never by mere chance; it is the result of forces working together. —James Cash Penney

Coachable Kids

Being coachable means your athlete is paying attention to other people who have the experience, wisdom, skills, and knowledge to help them improve their skills and become better athletes. Being coachable is an important life skill. Being coachable doesn't just apply to athletics; it applies to all areas in life.

Remember, coaches are authority figures and should be respected by both the parents and the athletes. Many times the way the player responds to a coach is in direct correlation to how the parent responds to the coach. If the parent does not respect the coach, normally the player will not be very coachable. This is why I strongly encourage parents to never say anything negative about the coach with your child present. If the parents downgrade the coach, more than likely the athlete will not respond well to that coach.

I realize all athletes are different, and many are more sensitive than others, but athletes who truly want to reach their full potential have to learn how to respond to criticism. They shouldn't pout, roll their eyes, or make excuses. They should look their coach in the eyes and listen to every word he or she says. They should respond to the coach with a "yes sir" or "yes ma'am," and try their best to do exactly as the coach instructed.

Humility is a very important trait in successful athletes. Humility is about opening yourself up to improvement and being coachable.

Athletes should admit that they are vulnerable in certain areas. Humble players are always trying to improve their game, whereas arrogant athletes think they already know everything and are not always open to being coached. This is why humble players continue to learn and improve and many times arrogant players regress.

Encourage your athlete to have a great attitude and be a sponge, gathering information. The athletes and coaches also should have open communication. It is important that you encourage your children from a young age to talk to the coach. The athlete should be the one to ask about practice time or for a game schedule, not the parent. If the athlete learns at an early age to create an open line of communication with the coach, it will eliminate issues as the athlete gets older.

The following are some evident traits of coachable athletes:

> They accept their role on the team.
> They are willing to accept the adjustments that need to be made.
> They have respect for authority.
> They are willing to make sacrifices for the improvement of the team.
> They are selfless.

My best skill was that I was coachable. I was a sponge and aggressive to learn. —Michael Jordan

Respecting Sports Officials

The way some parents act toward umpires, referees, and sports officials is out of control. Do sports officials make mistakes? Sure they do, but so do the players, coaches, and fans. We all make mistakes every day. Many times, for officials, if there is a close call, both teams expect it to go their way. Watch the crowd at a baseball or basketball game sometime. If the official makes a close call, the fans from one side of the stands will show their disapproval of the call. The next time a close call is made in favor of the other team, the other side of the stands will show their disapproval.

Unfortunately, there is a great shortage of officials. Frankly, it is no surprise that the retention rate is so low with the way many sports officials are treated. There is a 20 percent retention rate for sports officials past their third year. Many times sports directors are forced to hire less-experienced sports officials for higher-level venues, and the problem continues.

There are some parents who seem to enjoy heckling the officials. There are other parents who seem to jump on board and go along with the hecklers. Don't fall into that trap. Show good sportsmanship at all times. Many times when the parents and coaches show their dissatisfaction with the officials, it bleeds over to the players. The players start to lose their focus and composure, and obviously the loss of composure affects their performance in a negative way. Once the parents and coaches start arguing with the officials, the players have found an excuse in poor officiating for their lack of performance.

If your child is in athletics long enough, they are going to have plenty of officiating calls go against them. It is important that parents be strong role models for their children and teach them to have composure and stay focused on the task at hand.

You honor yourself by acting with dignity and composure.
—Allan Lokos

Finish What You Start

Should you allow your child to quit once they have signed up and committed to a sport? I think it's necessary that before your child commits to something, you sit down with them and communicate the importance of commitment and sticking with what they have decided to do. Kids need to understand that with athletics sometimes you will be inconvenienced, sometimes you will have tough practices, and sometimes your commitments to the team will have priority over something you would rather be doing at the time.

Many times young kids get into something, and it wasn't quite what they expected it to be. However, this is a life-lesson opportunity for parents. If the athletes don't learn to follow through with their commitment now, when they have the support system of their parents, how will they follow through as adults when they don't have a support system to encourage them? Young athletes should understand that challenging experiences build character, and taking the easy way out can sometimes become a habit.

Sports are full of ups and downs. In sports and in life you have to deal with both the highs and lows. Some kids are fine when they are successful, but when the tide turns and they are not successful, they don't want to participate anymore. I have had parents tell me their athletes are too competitive and can't handle losing. So when they lose, they want to quit. That is not competitive. That is quitting. A competitor can't wait until the next competition to give it another try.

If your child quits over a lack of playing time, they are missing out on a great learning opportunity. They should be encouraged to work harder to *earn* more playing time rather than just expect playing time. Many young athletes are accustomed to instant gratification. Teaching them the importance of working for something and earning the right for more playing time is the best way to handle the situation.

If your child wants to quit, try to figure out your child's reasons for wanting to do so. Problem-solve with them, and see if together you can come up with a resolution to the problem. It may be something you as the parent can adjust. Maybe you are putting too much pressure on your athlete.

Encourage them to stick it out through the season, and then you can evaluate the situation for the following season.

However, I have seen a few unusual situations throughout the years where it is probably best for everyone if the athlete decides to no longer remain on the team.

There's winning and there's losing, and in life both will happen. What is never acceptable to me is quitting.
—Magic Johnson

Hold Your Athlete Accountable

When I was a young parent, I started looking at successful athletes and how their parents treated them. The number one trait was they held their kids accountable. There was a reaction for every negative action. All behaviors had consequences. It is important that you as the parent support the coach's decision and let the wrongdoing of your athlete be experienced. Sometimes it is difficult to watch your athlete be disciplined by running laps, sitting out a game, or being suspended from the team. But actions have consequences, and you should support the authority figures (coach, umpires, school officials) and hold your child accountable for their actions. Athletics should be an extension of the things you have them value at home, such as integrity, good attitude, effort, and sportsmanship.

It seems twenty years ago kids did not want to go home and tell their parents about getting in trouble at school or practice. The kids knew they were likely to get in even more trouble once they were home and had to face their parents about getting in trouble at school. Today, however, it seems that many parents will defend their children without even knowing the details of why they are in trouble. When parents respond by defending their children immediately, many kids learn to take advantage of the situation. Parents should realize in the big picture they are doing their kids a disservice by not holding them accountable for their actions.

Instill the value of hard work and earning something rather than instilling entitlement in your athletes. If your athlete is not starting, encourage them to work harder and improve their skills. Not everyone is going to be a starter, not everyone is going to make the honor roll, not everyone is going to be on student council, and not everyone is going to be first chair in band. However, everyone can show persistence in pursuing what is important to them.

I think individual sports (track, wrestling, tennis, golf, gymnastics) are very beneficial for young athletes. Individual sports are the best teachers of accountability and humility. You, as the athlete, are responsible for your successes and failures. It teaches young athletes to take ownership of their results and actions. It is also important for your athlete to take ownership of their mistakes. Don't allow them to make excuses or point the finger, blaming others.

The most important quality I look for in a player is accountability. You've got to be accountable for who you are. It's too easy to blame things on someone else. — Lenny Wilkens

Give Them Some Independence

Although many young athletes have already started to develop vital mental skills, most are developed around the junior high to high school age. Skills such as goal setting, resilience, focus, and humility are all important for the athlete's continued success.

If you want to create an independent and confident young athlete, you need to let them solve their problems. Many times, parents want to protect their children from experiencing devastating emotions. However, intervening slows down their very valuable psychological and behavioral development. Once your athlete starts junior high, you should allow him or her more independence. More independence for the athlete also means more responsibility on their part. At this time they should start getting their own gear ready for practice and games. If they forget something, don't come to their rescue. If they have a conflict, encourage them to handle it. I know this process will be difficult for parents who have always handled their athletes' issues, but it is a must for them to mature into adults capable of dealing with issues and making good decisions on their own. They need to learn to be more responsible. It should be the athlete's responsibility to listen to the coach and know when practice will be or when the game has been rescheduled. Giving your athlete more independence and more responsibility will give your athlete the opportunity to start developing their mental skills. They should start to set goals for themselves. Self-discipline and self-motivation will improve at this time as well.

Obviously, parents should continue to provide encouragement and support but allow it to be their child's experience. In order for your child to gain all that athletics has to offer, allow them to experience the losses, the heartbreaks, the disappointments, the time on the bench, the consequences for bad decisions, and the setbacks. Encourage them to own the situation and work their way out. This is when they really start to learn and grow as young adults and athletes. A little extra independence can help in many ways. Many times parents who are overly involved can cause their athletes to struggle with anxiety. The athletes want to please their parents so much that they get nervous, and their performance is compromised. Anxiety can affect their performance by interfering with focus and confidence. A little breathing room can help the athlete mature socially and athletically.

The greatest gifts you can give your children are the roots of responsibility and the wings of independence.
—Denis Waitley

Shoot for the Stars

All athletes should be goal oriented. Goals give the athlete a road map. Setting goals allows you to see where you are and where you want to go. For many great athletes, goal setting and planning the path to achieve that goal is an everyday habit. When the goals are in place, the athletes become focused and self-motivated on achieving those goals. There will always be setbacks, and they will face plenty of adversity, but those who maintain their focus and continue to work toward their goals will be very successful.

The goals set by athletes should always be challenging but attainable. Young athletes should always go over their goals with a coach or parent to make sure the goals are realistic and are capable of being achieved. However, the goals should always be the athlete's goals and not goals set for them by their parents. If the goals are determined by a parent, the athlete will likely be much less motivated to achieve them. Self-motivation is one of the most important factors for athletes to be successful in achieving their goals.

Most young athletes (pre-junior high) set goals way too high, and many times they are not realistic. Obviously, it can be frustrating to set your goals way too high, put in a tremendous amount of work, and ultimately not be close to achieving those goals. This usually leads to the athletes quickly giving up on their goals.

It is also a good idea to do a skills inventory. The athletes should, determine what skills are important to the sport, and honestly grade themselves in each of the areas. Then they can go to work trying to improve in each of the important skill sets of their sport. They should not just focus on the areas where they are strongest. If the athletes only focus on their strengths, their weaknesses will likely be exploited by the competition. They should maximize their strengths and minimize their weaknesses.

It is very important that athletes write down their goals. Also they should write down the additional things they are going to have to do in order to achieve those goals. The athletes should remember that challenging goals will require them to get out of their comfort zone. Once they have finished, they should place a copy of the goals somewhere visible so they will see the sheet every day. This will be a daily reminder of the contract they have with themselves. As athletes they should have both long- term (one year or longer) and short-term goals. The short-term goals should align with their long-term goals. Their short-term goals should be used to pace their success (checkpoints) in working toward their long-term goals. They should understand that many times there will be setbacks, but that doesn't mean they compromise their goals. They should keep their eyes on the prize.

> *We need to know where we are going and how we plan to get there. Our dreams and aspirations must be translated into real and tangible goals with priorities and time frames.*
> —Merlin Olsen

Let Athletes Be Athletes

If your athlete is involved in multiple sports, is having fun, and is enjoying all of them, don't discourage them from participating in each sport, only to specialize in one. Many athletes are specializing in one sport at an early age in hopes of a college scholarship or a professional career. The increased time, cost, effort, and commitment is not a guarantee that a scholarship awaits the athlete in the future. Playing different sports and cross-training improves athleticism, prevents injuries, avoids burnout, and can be more enjoyable for the athlete. Many times this specialization comes from a dream the parents have for their child. Children who are forced into a single sport early in their athletic career are robbed of more varied athletic experiences that can be critical to developing overall athleticism.

When athletes do the same movements in the same sports year round, there will be an increase in injuries due to muscle fatigue. Muscle fatigue puts commonly used joints at risk for injury.

I would strongly encourage your young athlete to try as many sports as possible, and hopefully they will be successful at multiple sports. Being involved in multiple sports will make them better athletes overall. Multisport athletes are generally good decision makers and more creative athletes. Being involved in multiple sports will allow them to determine which sports best fit them. If an athlete only plays one sport, it should be their choice without any outside influences.

I think athletes should participate in multiple sports; however, I think it is important to only participate in one sport at a time. If an athlete is trying to play two sports during the same season, the athlete will not perform as well in either sport. Excelling in athletics takes a lot of focus and commitment, and obviously if an athlete is playing two sports during the same season, they will not be totally focused or committed to either one. This can cause a lot of frustration for the athlete because they may only be performing at 90 percent of their normal level.

As an athletic director at a small school, I have always strongly encouraged athletes to participate in multiple sports. This enables the school to be successful in all programs and allows athletes to be athletes. Athletes love to compete, and this gives them that opportunity.

> *The first questions I'll ask about a kid are "What other sports does he play? What does he do? What are his positions? Is he a big hitter in baseball? Is he a pitcher? Does he play hoops?" All of those things are important to me. I hate that kids don't play three sports in high school. I think that they should play year-round and get every bit of it that they can through that experience. I really, really don't favor kids having to specialize in one sport. Even at USC, I want to be the biggest proponent for two-sport athletes on the college level. I want guys that are so special athletically, and so competitive, that they can compete in more than one sport*
> *—Pete Carroll*

Transferable Skills

As discussed several times already, it is very important that our athletes are learning valuable life skills through athletics, such as teamwork, strong work ethic, resiliency, self-discipline, and focus. It is equally important that the athlete transfer these same skill sets to other areas in their life. Many times athletes will work hard and be disciplined in athletics, but they will not display the same traits in other areas. It should be unacceptable for a star basketball player who works very hard in the gym to not put forth the same effort in the classroom.

The wrestler should have the same work ethic, self-discipline, and focus in the classroom as he demonstrates on the mat. The softball player should show the same commitment to playing her instrument in the band as she does to the softball team. The high school football player should show the same level of teamwork to the choir as he does to the football team. We should demand a good effort and attitude from our athletes in all areas of their life. We should accept nothing less than their best effort in the classroom or a part-time job. Parents should always stress that their student athletes attack all of their activities with tenacity and passion.

Excellence is the gradual result of always striving to do better.
—*Pat Riley*

Confidence: I Don't Think I Can, I Know I Can

Confidence is developed over time. So going back to the goals, for each of the short-term (checkpoint) goals the athletes reach, the more confident they will become in achieving their overall goals.

For most athletes, the statement "the harder you work, the more confident you become" is true, but some athletes know they have worked hard and don't want to mess it up. So they compete to not lose, instead of competing to win. There is a big difference. If they are competing to win, they are making things happen by playing aggressively. Athletes who are competing to win know they are going to make mistakes throughout the competition, but they stay focused and compete from whistle to whistle. They expect success for themselves and their team. The ones who are competing to not lose are more passive because their focus is on never making a mistake.

With this said, the best way to develop confidence is by being extremely prepared. If athletes know they have trained harder and smarter than their competition, it develops a level of confidence that gives them a competitive edge. Putting in the work gives them the confidence to accept challenges instead of fearing defeat or worrying about a poor performance.

Confident athletes don't think they are going to be successful; they *know* they are going to be. This type of athlete fails just like we all do, but they have a short memory. They stay focused on their goals even though they have setbacks. Confidence is the energy that drives success.

One important key to success is self-confidence. An important key to self-confidence is preparation.
—Arthur Ashe

Encourage Leadership

Players who have a good attitude and a strong work ethic make the best leaders. They are leading by example each day. The best way for a parent to create a good leader in their athlete is by demonstrating character in their everyday life. Out of all the lessons you can teach a child, being of strong character is the most important. An athlete who can learn the foundation of trust, honesty, respect, and integrity—and incorporate those qualities in their everyday life—will be ready for a lifetime of successful leadership.

Give your athlete experiences that will teach them about diversity and inclusion, and encourage them to view all of their teammates as important participants of the team. Some additional qualities of strong leaders are the following:

1. Good leaders have composure. They stay cool in stressful situations. A leader believes all problems have solutions.
2. Good leaders are authentic. Their leadership is not an act. They are genuine on and off the field.
3. They lead in times of success, and they lead even better in times of stress.
4. Good leaders don't blame or point fingers. They take ownership and expect others to take ownership as well. They hold themselves accountable and are humble.
5. They make everyone around them better.

6. They lead by example. They may be good vocal leaders, but the best ones always lead by example as well.
7. The leadership must be in line with the team goals or the mission of the school. The leader must be a good communicator, constantly reminding the players of the team's mission.
8. Good leaders respect teammates at all times. If athletes are going to receive respect, it is important that they also give respect.
9. Positive energy is better than negative energy every time. Leaders have to get people to buy in. It is difficult if they are using negative energy. If they are trying to persuade a teammate to do something by using negative energy, the player may do what they want, but they may not want to. Leaders have to make them want to do the right thing. The best way is through positive energy.
10. Followers will have confidence in a good leader, but a great leader makes the followers have confidence in themselves.
11. Good leaders connect to the individual. To get the most out of individuals, you have to make a connection and create a relationship with them.

If your actions inspire others to dream more, learn more, do more, and become more, you are a leader.
—John Quincy Adams

Body Language Speaks Loudly

Parents and athletes should know that the way athletes carry themselves is very important. Athletes have been trained to have a good attitude, so many times they don't say anything negative with their mouth, but their body language speaks volumes about their attitude.

An athlete's body language shows their character. How do they respond to criticism? How do they respond when they are standing on the sidelines or sitting on the bench? How do they respond after they make a mistake? How do they respond when a teammate makes an error? Do they roll their eyes, pout, point a finger at a teammate, and/or throw their arms up in frustration? This is all negative body language and speaks volumes about the athlete.

Maintaining positive body language during a game is critical. If a defensive back gets beaten on a pass play and walks back to his position with his head down, an observant coach for the opposing team is likely to pick on the same defensive back in the next few plays. A baseball coach is likely to pick up on a pitcher struggling and showing his emotions with his body language by having his players take every pitch (not swinging) until the batter gets behind in the count. A basketball player may throw her hands up in frustration after her teammate passes the ball out of bounds. This type of body language speaks the same as yelling at your teammate, "Come on, can't you do anything?" Usually coaches are very good at reading body language, so negative body language can lead to the player's coach sitting the player out, or the opposing coach taking advantage of the frustrated player.

Negative body language can represent laziness, poor sportsmanship, negative attitude, and frustration. Positive body language can represent excitement, confidence, composure, and determination.

You can tell a lot by someone's body language.
—Harvey Wolter

Little Things Make a Big Difference

Little things done right over time will add up to make a big difference in developing your athlete's abilities. Sometimes mastering skills can become monotonous, but obviously it requires drill after drill at practice after practice, day after day. However, the mastery of the small skill sets will make a big difference in your athlete's ability to perform at an elite level.

Many high school athletes work very hard at getting into shape and developing their skills. Yet all of that hard work can be counterproductive if they don't take care of their bodies by eating right and getting the appropriate amount of sleep. Nutrition can help enhance athletic performance. Following a good diet can help provide the energy they need to compete up to their ability. They are likely to become tired and perform poorly during sports when they do not get the appropriate amount of nutrition. Getting the right amount of sleep and rest is also critical for maximizing the athletic performance. If they are not getting enough sleep, their reaction time will not be as effective as it would otherwise. Make sure your athletes are eating right and getting plenty of sleep.

Today's top-level competitors in all sports are so good and so equal in ability that many times it is the ones who are doing the small things right that will establish a competitive edge over their competition.

Eating right, getting the appropriate amount of sleep, getting a good warm-up, being focused, and having composure can all make a difference. The small things can make a big difference when the difference between success and failure is often one point, or one inch, or 1/100th of a second.

Greatness is a lot of small things done well. — Eric Thomas

Controlling Emotions

Some athletes have the magical ability to always perform their best when it matters the most. That ability seems magical, but most of the time it is actually the ability to block out all distractions and focus totally on the task at hand. The magic is in their ability to master their emotions. Great composure enables the athlete to avoid getting sidetracked when the official makes a questionable call, when an opponent elbows them intentionally, or when the opposing fans are heckling them. Athletes who are able to control their emotions will give themselves a big competitive advantage. There are many highs and lows in athletics, and many times it can be an emotional rollercoaster. Athletes can go from hero to zero from one play to the next. It is important for athletes to be able to maintain their focus and composure throughout this process.

In order for your athlete to maintain their composure in competition, they must accept that they are going to make mistakes and experience setbacks when competing. They should remember that they are human, and they can't be perfect. They should learn to accept their mistakes and move on so they can make the next play.

Many times the way the player deals with emotions such as frustration, anxiety, and anger is the exact way they see their parents deal with those emotions. So parents should always try to model composure in their daily life and stay positive in dealing with difficult situations.

For most athletes anxiety and nerves are a big distraction. Explain to your athlete, "Nerves are your friend. Being nervous means you have increased adrenaline, and increased adrenaline gives you extra energy to compete at a higher level." Here are some other suggestions to help manage anxiety:

Visualization is one method athletes can use to increase their focus and decrease their anxiety. Visualization involves the athletes imagining themselves performing their athletic tasks to perfection prior to the athletic event. Visualization allows the athletes to break down their responsibilities in their mind. By seeing themselves succeed at the tasks time and time again, it will increase the probability of it being performed that way in a live-action situation.

Self-talk is another method that increases focus and helps eliminate anxiety. Self-talk is just that. Athletes repeat positive affirmations or statements to themselves over and over until they believe it will happen.

Every great player has learned the two Cs:
how to concentrate and how to maintain composure.
—Bryon Nelson

Thinking before Reacting

Take some time to think about the following situations and determine which scenario would provide the best learning opportunity for your athletes:

Scenario 1: Three athletes are on the same softball team. They lose their game by one run. The game ended when one of their players was called out at home plate. When the athletes were discussing the game with their parents, Parent 1 said, "It's okay, Sarah; the umpire was terrible. You guys were cheated out of that game." Player 1 learns to take zero responsibility and to blame others when things don't go her way. Parent 2 says, "Lisa, why did you strike out twice and miss that ground ball? Were you even trying?" Player 2's confidence takes a big hit, and she thinks it's her fault they lost the game. Parent 3 waits a while and then approaches his daughter and says, "Good effort, keep working, and the next time we will get that team." Player 3 learns persistence. She learns that if she continues to work hard and smart, the results will be better in the future.

Scenario 2: Three athletes were suspended for one game from their high school football team for breaking team policy. The rules and consequences were made very clear to the parents and athletes during the preseason parent meeting. Parent 1 says, "You should just quit; you won't get to play when you return anyway." Player 1 learns to quit when things don't go his way, even though it was the result of his own bad decision. Parent 2 says, "It was the coach's fault. We will get a lawyer and fight it." Player 2 learns to blame someone else and not take any ownership of the wrongdoing. Parent 3 says, "You need to learn from your mistakes. When you return, you will need to work really hard and have a better attitude than ever before to win back the respect of your teammates and coaches." Player 3 learns accountability and the importance of being a teammate.

Scenario 3: Three players have worked very hard for their high school basketball team, but they have not obtained a starting role. All three players come off the bench and contribute to the team, but they feel they should be starting so they seek advice from their parents. Parent 1 says, "I can't believe Jimmy Johnson is starting before you. He is terrible. The coach is playing favoritism." Player 1 learns that it is someone else's fault, and it is okay to talk negatively about other players and the coach. Parent 2 says, "I am going straight to the athletic director Monday, and if that doesn't work, I'm going to get on the agenda for the next school board meeting." Player 2 learns improper protocol and not to take responsibility for the situation. Parent 3 says, "I know you have worked hard, and I'm very proud of you. You have an important role on the team. You should visit with Coach Wilson after practice about the situation, but you need to accept what he says and continue to work hard and have a good attitude." Player 3 learns persistence, accountability, and how to talk to an adult authority figure in an appropriate way.

If we asked which parent handled each situation the best in order to produce a well-adjusted adult, everyone would be able to answer the question correctly. However, all three scenarios are handled like parents 1 and 2 handled them every day. Many parents get caught up in the emotions of athletics to the point that they do not make appropriate decisions. As a parent it is important that you think before you react. Always think of the message you are sending your child through your conversation.

What happens is not as important as how you react to what happens. —Ellen Glasgow

Do the Math

Many parents spend a tremendous amount of money chasing a college scholarship. Obviously you should have high expectations for your children, and you should support and encourage them to pursue their goals, but you should also understand the facts. Approximately, 2 percent of high school athletes will receive athletic scholarships from NCAA colleges and universities. Many of those scholarships will only be partial scholarships. Would parents be better off saving the money they spend on traveling teams, trainers, showcases, and going to national tournaments, and just pay for their athlete's education? Another option would be to invest the money in a tutor. The overall odds are much better for getting an academic scholarship over an athletic scholarship.

You can also factor in that most college student athletes will spend about twenty-five to thirty hours a week focusing on their sport. If they were to obtain a part-time job working twenty-five to thirty hours a week, they might be way ahead. So, is the athletic scholarship worth pursuing? Obviously that depends on the family and the situation. I had one son attend the University of Oklahoma on a wrestling scholarship. The great experience he gained through competing and the lifelong friends that he made through the process, plus the joy of watching him compete, was worth every cent and then some. The same can be said for my youngest son who played two years of baseball at Northern Oklahoma College. He had a great experience that was well worth it. He is currently playing baseball at the University of Central Oklahoma, and I'm sure he will have a great experience there as well.

Also, I know there are many reasons for choosing a certain college, and the cost is not always the main factor. However, many times cost is a considerable factor in choosing a particular college. So it is important to know the bottom line, or the final cost per year. Many times the scholarship offered can be deceiving. For example, an athlete may receive a partial scholarship of 25 percent to attend College A. College A has a tuition cost of $8,000/year. College B offers a 75 percent scholarship, but the tuition for College B is $50,000/year. Many people hear the percentages and naturally think the 75 percent scholarship is the better opportunity, and it may be. However, if the out-of-pocket money is the main concern, College A would be the better situation for the athlete:

> For College A, $8,000 x .25 = $2,000 scholarship. So the total cost for tuition would be $8,000 - $2,000 = $6,000.

> For College B, $50,000 x .75 = $37,500 scholarship. So the total cost for tuition would be $50,000 - $37,500 = $12,500.

The point is don't focus so much on obtaining the scholarship. If your athlete is doing all the right things (working hard and smart), and he or she is talented, the opportunities are likely to be there. The most important thing is to enjoy the journey. If the opportunity of a college scholarship doesn't present itself, the family should still enjoy the journey.

The prize is in the process. — Baron Baptiste

What Are College Coaches Looking For?

It is very important for parents and their athletes to know exactly what recruiters are looking for. If coaches come to an athletic event to watch an athlete play, they are looking for far more than just the athlete's skills on the playing field. They will watch the athlete in pregame to see how they interact with their teammates and what their intensity level is as they go through drills. During the game, they will be interested in how the athlete responds to adversity, their leadership skills on the field, and if they compete hard all the time. We all know that the athlete's talent level is very important in the college recruiting process, but there are many other traits that are extremely important as well.

1. Academics. College coaches are looking for students who are academically sound. They want student athletes who are genuinely concerned about their grades. Remember, they will be reluctant to invest a scholarship in an athlete they think may not make the cut academically.
2. Character. College coaches are looking for student athletes with outstanding character who will always represent their university with class. Strong character improves the chances of the athlete having a successful college experience.
3. Work ethic. At the college level, everyone is talented. The separation in the athletes will come from their work ethic.

Also, student athletes will have to have a strong work ethic in order to balance their athletic success with their academic success.
4. Reliable. College coaches want athletes they can depend on. They are looking for students who will always show up when they are supposed to and do what they are supposed to do.
5. Competitive. College coaches are looking for athletes who are ultracompetitive—they love the challenge of competition. Many great athletes are not great competitors. Those who are not great competitors will struggle in college, where all athletes are good. Competitiveness is like work ethic; it is something that separates college athletes. Many college coaches also like multisport athletes because they are usually great competitors.
6. Coachable. College coaches are looking for athletes who want to be coached. The coaches want athletes who have a desire to improve technically, tactically, mentally, and physically.
7. Leader. Many college coaches look for leadership qualities in their recruits. They want student athletes who are capable of leading their teammates in a positive way on and off the field.
8. Team player. College coaches are looking for team players. They are interested in players who will commit to the team and the team goals.
9. Mentally tough. College coaches want players who are focused, aggressive, and play hard all the time. They look for players who are fearless and don't let mistakes influence their game.

Obviously, there will be other important traits that college coaches will look for depending on the sport and their needs at the time. Many times the coaches will contact the potential athlete's high school coaches and ask them questions about the traits listed above. Also, it is important to know that most of the time the coach or a college representative (someone from the athletic department) will check out the potential athlete's social media pages during this process. Remember, they want to recruit high-character athletes.

Act right all the time because someone is always watching.
—Gwen Ifill

Start Thinking about College

If your student athlete has the ability and desire to participate in athletics at the college level, it is important that both parents and athletes are proactive in the process.

The following is a list of tasks your athlete can do and a timeline in which to do them to make sure he or she is prepared through the NCAA Clearinghouse.

Grade 9

* Ask their counselor for a list of their high school's NCAA core courses to make sure they take the right classes.

Grade 10

* Register with the NCAA Eligibility Center at eligibilitycenter.org.

Grade 11

* Check with their counselor to make sure they will graduate on time with the required number of NCAA core courses.
* Take the ACT or SAT, and submit their scores to the NCAA using code 9999.
* At the end of the year, ask their counselor to upload their official transcript to the NCAA Eligibility Center.

Grade 12

* Finish their last NCAA core courses.
* Take the ACT or SAT again, if necessary, and submit their scores to the NCAA using code 9999.
* Complete all academic and amateurism questions in their NCAA Eligibility Center account at eligibilitycenter.org.
* After they graduate, ask their counselor to submit their final official transcript with proof of graduation to the NCAA Eligibility Center.

The greatest pleasure in life is doing what people say you cannot do. —Walter Bagehot

Scholarship Information

There are only six sports that offer full-ride scholarships. The six sports are football, men's basketball, women's basketball, women's gymnastics, tennis, and volleyball. There are approximately 150,000 scholarships available for Division I and Division II sports. There are about 8 million high school athletes.

All six of these sports (football, basketball, women's gymnastics, tennis, and volleyball) offer what are called head-count scholarships. An athlete who receives a Division I scholarship in these sports receives a full ride.

In Division I men's basketball, thirteen student athletes will receive a full-ride scholarship, and all other players on the team will not receive any athletic money. All of the scholarships given out are full rides. They are not divided into partial scholarships.

The other NCAA athletic programs are considered equivalency sports. Under an equivalency system, the NCAA dictates the maximum number of scholarships allowed per sport, but full rides aren't required. So most of the time, these scholarships are divided into many partial scholarships. For example, a Division I wrestling team is allotted 9.9 scholarships, but it may have thirty-two wrestlers on the team. The coach can divide the 9.9 scholarships any way he chooses among the thirty-two members of the team.

It is important to know that many of the Division I sports teams do not offer the maximum amount of scholarships permitted by the NCAA because some schools can't afford it.

It is also important to note that athletic scholarships are renewed each year, and just because your athlete received a 30 percent scholarship in year one doesn't mean he or she will receive the same amount in year two. They could receive less, but they could also receive more.

What I tell student athletes is first of all, you've made good choices this far in order to be able to be in college and to be an athlete. Keep making good choices. — Condoleezza Rice

College Athletic Scholarship Limits for Men 2018–19

College athletic associations set the maximum number of athletic scholarships their member schools can award to student athletes for the official sports. Here are the limits per sport for the 2018–19 year for men's varsity sports:

	NCAA I	NCAA II	NAIA	NJCAA
Baseball	11.7	9	12	24
Basketball	13	10		15
Basketball–NAIA I			11	
Basketball–NAIA II			6	
Bowling				12
Cross Country–NCAA limits include Track and Field	12.6	12.6	5	10
Fencing	4.5	4.5		
Football–NCAA I FBS	85			
Football–NCAA I FCS	63			
Football–Other divisions		36	24	85
Golf	4.5	3.6	5	8
Gymnastics	6.3	5.4		
Ice Hockey	18	13.5		16
Lacrosse	12.6	10.8		20

Rifle–includes women on coed teams	3.6	3.6		
Skiing	6.3	6.3		
Soccer	9.9	9	12	24
Swimming and Diving	9.9	8.1	8	15
Tennis	4.5	4.5	5	9
Track and Field–NCAA limits include Cross Country	12.6	12.6	12	20
Volleyball	4.5	4.5		
Water Polo	4.5	4.5		
Wrestling	9.9	9	8	20

College Athletic Scholarship Limits for Women 2018–19

College athletic associations set the maximum number of athletic scholarships their member schools can award to student athletes for the official sports. Here are the limits per sport for the 2018–19 year for women's varsity sports:

	NCAA I	NCAA II	NAIA	NJCAA
Basketball	15	10		15
Basketball–NAIA I			11	
Basketball–NAIA II			6	
Beach Volleyball	6	5		10
Bowling	5	5		12
Cross Country–NCAA limits include Track and Field	18	12.6	5	10
Equestrian	15	15		
Fencing	5	4.5		
Field Hockey	12	6.3		
Golf	6	5.4	5	8
Gymnastics	12	6		
Ice Hockey	18	18		
Lacrosse	12	9.9		20

Rifle–includes men on coed teams	3.6	3.6		
Rowing	20	20		
Rugby	12	12		
Skiing	7	6.3		
Soccer	14	9.9	12	24
Softball	12	7.2	10	24
Swimming and Diving	14	8.1	8	15
Tennis	8	6	5	9
Track and Field–NCAA limits include Cross Country	18	12.6	12	20
Triathlon	6.5	5		
Volleyball	12	8	8	14
Water Polo	8	8		

Education is the passport to the future, for tomorrow belongs to those who prepare for it today.
—Malcolm X

NCAA Division I Academic Requirements

To be eligible to compete in NCAA sports during the first year at a Division I school, the athlete must graduate from high school and meet *all* of the following requirements:

* Complete sixteen core courses.
    - Four years of English
    - Three years of math (Algebra 1 or higher)
    - Two years of natural/physical sciences (including one year of lab science if your high school offers it)
    - One additional year of English, math, or natural/physical science
    - Two years of social science
    - Four additional years of English, math, natural/physical science, social science, foreign language, comparative religion, or philosophy

* Complete ten core courses, including seven in English, math, or natural/physical science, before your seventh semester. Once you begin your seventh semester, you may not repeat or replace any of those ten courses to improve your core-course GPA.

* Earn at least a 2.3 GPA in your core courses.

* Earn an SAT combined score or ACT sum score matching your core-course GPA on the Division I sliding scale, which balances your test score and core-course GPA. If you have a low test score, you will need a higher core-course GPA to be eligible. If you have a low core-course GPA, you will need a higher test score to be eligible.

NCAA Division I Sliding Scale

Core GPA	SAT	ACT
3.550 and above	400	37
3.525	410	38
3.500	420	39
3.475	430	40
3.450	440	41
3.425	450	41
3.400	460	42
3.375	470	42
3.350	480	43
3.325	490	44
3.300	500	44
3.275	510	45
3.250	520	46
3.225	530	46
3.200	540	47
3.175	550	47
3.150	560	48
3.125	570	49
3.100	580	49
3.075	590	50
3.050	600	50

NCAA DIVISION I ACADEMIC REQUIREMENTS

3.025	610	51
3.000	620	52
2.975	630	52
2.950	640	53
2.925	650	53
2.900	660	54
2.875	670	55
2.850	680	56
2.825	690	56
2.800	700	57
2.775	710	58
2.750	720	59
2.725	730	60
2.700	740	61
2.675	750	61
2.650	760	62
2.625	770	63
2.600	780	64
2.575	790	65
2.550	800	66
2.525	810	67
2.500	820	68
2.475	830	69
2.450	840	70
2.425	850	70
2.400	860	71
2.375	870	72
2.350	880	73
2.325	890	74

If you have not met all of the Division I academic requirements, you may not compete in your first year at college. However, if you qualify as an academic redshirt, you may practice during your first term in college and receive an athletic scholarship for the entire year.

To qualify as an academic redshirt, you must graduate from high school and meet all of the following academic requirements:

* Complete sixteen core courses.
    - Four years of English
    - Three years of math (Algebra 1 or higher)
    - Two years of natural/physical science (including one year of lab science if your high school offers it)
    - One additional year of English, math, or natural/physical science
    - Two years of social science
    - Four additional years of English, math, natural/physical science, social science, foreign language, comparative religion, or philosophy

* Earn at least a 2.0 GPA in your core courses.

* Earn an SAT combined score or ACT sum score matching your core-course GPA on the Division I sliding scale.

GPAs Below 2.3 Are Redshirt Only

2.300	900	75
2.299	910	76
2.275	910	76
2.250	920	77
2.225	930	78
2.200	940	79
2.175	950	80
2.150	960	81
2.125	970	82

2.100	980	83
2.075	990	84
2.050	1000	85
2.025	1010	86
2.000	1020	86

Develop a passion for learning. If you do, you will never cease to grow. —Anthony J. D'Angelo

NCAA Division II Academic Requirements

To be eligible to compete in NCAA sports during your first year at a Division II school, you must meet academic requirements for your core courses, grade-point average (GPA), and test scores.

You must graduate from high school and meet all of the following requirements:

* Complete sixteen core courses.
  - Three years of English
  - Two years of math (Algebra I or higher)
  - Two years of natural or physical science (including one year of lab science if your high school offers it)
  - Three additional years of English, math, or natural or physical science
  - Two years of social science
  - Four additional years of English, math, natural or physical science, social science, foreign language, comparative religion, or philosophy

* Earn at least a 2.2 GPA in your core courses.

* Earn an SAT combined score or ACT sum score matching your core-course GPA on the Division II sliding scale, which balances

NCAA DIVISION II ACADEMIC REQUIREMENTS

your test score and core-course GPA. If you have a low test score, you need a higher core-course GPA to be eligible. If you have a low core-course GPA, you need a higher test score to be eligible.

NCAA Division II Sliding Scale

Use for Division II Full Qualifier after August 1, 2018			Use for Division II Partial Qualifier after August 1, 2018		
Core GPA	SAT	ACT	Core GPA	SAT	ACT
3.300 and above	400	37	3.050 and above	400	37
3.275	410	38	3.025	410	38
3.250	420	39	3.000	420	39
3.225	430	40	2.975	430	40
3.200	440	41	2.950	440	41
3.175	450	41	2.925	450	41
3.150	460	42	2.900	460	42
3.125	470	42	2.875	470	42
3.100	480	43	2.850	480	43
3.075	490	44	2.825	490	44
3.050	500	44	2.800	500	44
3.025	510	45	2.775	510	45
3.000	520	46	2.750	520	46
2.975	530	46	2.725	530	46
2.950	540	47	2.700	540	47
2.925	550	47	2.675	550	47
2.900	560	48	2.650	560	48
2.875	570	49	2.625	570	49
2.850	580	49	2.600	580	49
2.825	590	50	2.575	590	50
2.800	600	50	2.550	600	50

2.775	610	51	2.525	610	51
2.750	620	52	2.500	620	52
2.725	630	52	2.475	630	52
2.700	640	53	2.450	640	53
2.675	650	53	2.425	650	53
2.650	660	54	2.400	660	54
2.625	670	55	2.375	670	55
2.600	680	56	2.350	680	56
2.575	690	56	2.325	690	56
2.550	700	57	2.300	700	57
2.525	710	58	2.275	710	58
2.500	720	59	2.250	720	59
2.475	730	59	2.225	730	60
2.450	740	60	2.200	740	61
2.425	750	61	2.175	750	61
2.400	760	62	2.150	760	62
2.375	770	63	2.125	770	63
2.350	780	64	2.100	780	64
2.325	790	65	2.075	790	65
2.300	800	66	2.050	800	66
2.275	810	67	2.025	810	67
2.250	820	68	2.000	820 and above	68 and above
2.225	830	69			
2.200	840 and above	70 and above			

If you enroll full-time at a Division II school, and you have not met all the Division II academic requirements, you may not compete in your first year. However, if you meet the requirements to be a partial qualifier, you may practice and receive an athletic scholarship in your first year at college. To be a partial qualifier,

NCAA DIVISION II ACADEMIC REQUIREMENTS

you must graduate from high school and meet all of the following requirements:

* Complete sixteen core courses.
    - Three years of English
    - Two years of math (Algebra I or higher)
    - Two years of natural or physical science (including one year of lab science if your high school offers it)
    - Three additional years of English, math, or natural or physical science
    - Two years of social science
    - Four additional years of English, math, natural or physical science, social science, foreign language, comparative religion, or philosophy

* Earn at least a 2.0 GPA in your core courses.

* Earn an SAT combined score or ACT sum score matching your core-course GPA on the Division II sliding scale.

Education comes from within; you get it by struggle and effort and thought. —Napoleon Hill

NCAA Division III

Division III schools *do not* offer athletic scholarships. Seventy-five percent of Division III student athletes receive some form of merit or need-based financial aid. If you are planning to attend a Division III school, you do not need to register with the NCAA Eligibility Center. Division III schools set their own admission standards.

Success is where preparation and opportunity meet.
—Bobby Unser

NAIA Academic Requirements

To qualify for an NAIA school, a student athlete must graduate from high school and meet two out of the three following requirements.

- Achieve a minimum overall GPA of 2.0 on a 4.0 scale.
- Graduate in the top half of your high school class.
- Achieve the NAIA minimum test score requirements:

    * Composite score of 18 on the ACT*
    ** Exception: ACT tests taken March 1, 2016 through April 30, 2019 require a composite score of 16.
    * A score of 970 on the SAT (Evidence-Based Reading and Writing and Math)
    ** Exception: SAT tests taken March 1, 2016 through April 30, 2019 require a score of 860.

Education is the foundation upon which we build our future.
—Christine Gregoire

NJCAA Academic Requirements

In order to meet the NJCAA academic eligibility requirements, an athlete must graduate from high school or receive a GED that has been authorized by a state-recognized education agency or a regional association or approved by the NJCAA National Office.

Sports build good habits, confidence, and discipline. They make players into community leaders and teach them how to strive for a goal, handle mistakes, and cherish growth opportunities.
—Julie Foudy

All Sports Experiences Will End Sooner or Later

The final buzzer of every sports career will go off at some point, and hopefully you as a parent and your child will be left with many great memories. Athletics should be such a great learning experience for the student athletes; however, the learning experiences gained hinges on the parents being positive, encouraging, guiding, and even demonstrating a little tough love at times. The athletes should be able to draw from their experiences as an athlete and apply them to their new challenges throughout life.

The job of an athlete's parent is a tough one, and it takes a lot of effort to do it well. Parents—like athletes, coaches, and officials—are going to make mistakes in dealing with children in athletics. Realizing you have made a mistake and trying to right the wrong is the important part. If you continue to make the same mistake, it will ultimately negatively affect the child you are trying to help. Unfortunately, there are no do-overs in raising your children, so it is critical that you make good decisions and raise them to make good decisions as well.

I have learned that raising children is the single most difficult thing in the world to do. It takes hard work, love, luck, and a lot of energy, and it is the most rewarding experience that you can ever have. —Janet Reno

Lightning Source UK Ltd.
Milton Keynes UK
UKHW040809270219
338083UK00011B/557/P